AMAZING HISTORY

BURIED TREASURE

JOHN MALAM

A+

Smart Apple Media

Published by Smart Apple Media
2140 Howard Drive West
North Mankato, MN 56003

Created by Q2A Media
Series Editor: Jean Coppendale
Designers: Diksha Khatri, Ashita Murgai
Picture Researchers: Lalit Dalal, Jyoti Sachdev
Illustrators: Hemant Arya, Adil A Siddiqui, Amir Khan

Picture credits
t=top b=bottom c=center l=left r=right m=middle
Cover images: Mel Fisher's Treasures Archives: b
Back cover: Julia Chernikova/ Shutterstock: tr
Scubabartek/ Dreamstime.com: 4b, REUTERS/ Ho New: 5b, Images&Stories, photographersdirect.com: 6br,
The Bridgeman Art Library: 7t, 18m, Mel Fisher's Treasures Archives: 8bl, 8br, www.hmsedinburgh.co.uk: 9t,
Imagestate Ltd/ Photlibrary: 10b, Library and Archives Canada: 11t, Julia Chernikova/ Shutterstock: 12t, Ron Watts/
Corbis: 13b, Q2A Media: 14b, 22b, Rich Bartell/ Shutterstock: 16t, The Trustees of the British Museum: 19t, 29b,
Vladimir Korostyshevskiy/ Shutterstock: 23t, Robert Harding Picture Library Ltd/ Photolibrary: 24b,
University of Pennsylvania: 26b, DHuss/ Istockphoto: 27b, Akivi33/ Dreamstime.com: 28b.

Printed in the United States of America

The Library of Congress has cataloged the hardcover edition as follows:

Malam, John, 1957–
Buried Treasure / by John Malam.
p. cm. — (Amazing history)
Includes index
ISBN 978-1-59920-107-8 (hardcover)
ISBN 978-1-59920-208-2 (pbk)
1. Treasure troves—Juvenile literature. I. Title.

G525.M2235 2007
930.1—dc22 2007019361

9 8 7 6 5 4 3 2

Contents

What is buried treasure?

There is something magical about **treasure**. Under the ground, in secret **tombs**, or at the bottom of the sea, hidden treasure is waiting for people to find it.

Raiders of the past

Treasure hunters have been hard at work all over the world for thousands of years. Wherever they have been, they have left signs of their work. For example, in Egypt, the tombs of the ancient **pharaohs** are empty because thieves broke in and stole their treasure. But they missed one amazing tomb, and its treasure was found only a few years ago (see page 12).

Empty tomb

The pyramid of Pharaoh Khafre, built in about 2530 B.C., was raided many years ago

Ancient Egyptian tomb raiders stole the treasure from inside the pyramids.

Shipwreck treasure

The seabed is littered with the wrecks of ships, and many sank, taking their valuable cargoes with them. Ancient Greek and Roman ships were lost in the Mediterranean Sea. Then in the sixteenth century, heavy Spanish treasure ships sank as they sailed from South America to Europe. In the seas around China, there are many wrecks filled with fragile **porcelain**. But shipwrecks hold more than just treasure—they are like time capsules that show what life was like on the day they sank.

HOT SPOTS

A ship called the Geldermalsen smashed into a reef in 1752, on its way from China to Holland. In 1986, its cargo of thousands of pieces of Chinese porcelain sold for $15 million.

Precious porcelain
Chinese dishes and bowls found on the wreck look almost as good as new

Thousands of pieces of Chinese porcelain were lost when the *Royal Nanhai* sank more than 400 years ago.

King's gold

Archaeologists have discovered many fabulous treasures. Some of these wonderful things may have belonged to ancient kings, which makes them even more precious.

Treasure of Troy

In 1873, the archaeologist Heinrich Schliemann found a stunning treasure in Turkey. He uncovered gold cups and headdresses and silver objects that were 4,500 years old. Convinced that he had found the ancient city of Troy, Schliemann called it Priam's Treasure, after a king of Troy. He smuggled the treasure to Germany, but it disappeared in 1945. It was later found in 1993 in a museum in Russia.

Sophia Schliemann wearing gold jewelry discovered by her husband at Troy.

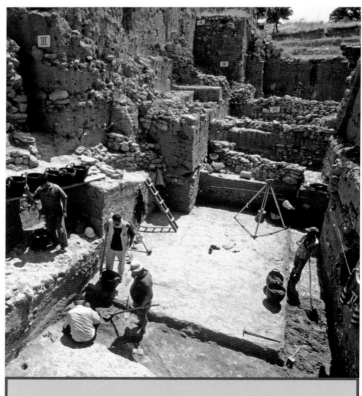

Archaeologists are still digging at Troy, revealing the ruins of ancient buildings.

Star symbol
This is the emblem of the royal family of King Philip II

This chest from the royal tomb at Vergina is made from 23 pounds (11 kg) of pure gold.

HOT SPOTS

King Philip was buried with one of his wives. Her remains were found in a solid gold box with a small gold crown, or diadem, of **myrtle** *leaves. This crown is considered to be one of the most beautiful pieces of jewelry in ancient history.*

King Philip's chest of gold

In 1977, as archaeologists dug away the soil of a huge **burial mound** in Vergina, in northern Greece, they discovered a royal tomb. The tomb was for King Philip II, father of Alexander the Great. His body had been **cremated**, and his ashes placed inside a magnificent chest of solid gold. The king had been buried with his armor and weapons, and the walls of the tomb were decorated with paintings. It was just as it had been left 2,300 years ago.

Treasure ships

Many ships ended their days as wrecks at the bottom of the sea, and some have gone to their watery graves loaded with valuable treasure.

Spanish gold

In 1622, the Spanish **galleon** *Atocha* sank off the coast of Florida. The ship was sailing from South America to Spain, loaded with a cargo of gold and silver bars and 250,000 silver coins. The king of Spain ordered a search, but the *Atocha* was never found. However, Mel Fisher, an American treasure hunter, eventually struck gold. In 1985, he located the wreck, and much of the treasure has been sold for millions of dollars.

NORTH
AMERICA

Florida

Mexico

A diver holding a gold ingot he found from the wreck of the *Atocha*.

Gold bars
Some **ingots** measure 8 x 1 inches (198 x 25mm)

Gold and silver treasure from the *Atocha* treasure ship.

Well-armed
The ship carried 12 big guns, 8 machine guns, and torpedoes

Fast mover
HMS *Edinburgh* was a light cruiser and could reach a speed of 32 knots, or 37 miles (59 km) per hour

HMS *Edinburgh* carried 93 wooden boxes loaded with bars of gold. In 1942, the gold was worth $3.75 million.

Torpedoed treasure

In 1942, the British warship HMS *Edinburgh* set sail from Russia with 465 bars of Russian gold. On the way to Britain, the ship was torpedoed by a German submarine and sank in the Barents Sea. It was not until 1981, in a daring **salvage operation**, that British diver Keith Jessop recovered most of the gold from a depth of 800 feet (245 m). It was worth more than $85 million. The treasure was shared between the British and Russian authorities and the people who had paid for the expedition. Jessop's reward was $4 million.

Barents Sea

Russia

Missing millions

Some buried treasure is still a mystery—no one really knows if it exists or not. Some people have spent years searching, but so far, have failed to find it.

Alaric's treasure

In A.D. 410, Rome was attacked by an army from Germany led by Alaric. His soldiers are said to have gathered the city's treasure before heading south through Italy. On the way, Alaric died. Legend says that he was buried with the treasure in the bed of the Busento River in southern Italy, and then the river flowed over his grave. Some people think this is only a story and there never was a treasure, but this has not stopped treasure hunters from searching for it.

EUROPE

Italy

Busento River

Leaders of the ancient world were often buried with great wealth, so there may be some truth in the story of Alaric's burial.

Stolen riches
Alaric is buried, surrounded by treasure stolen from the city of Rome

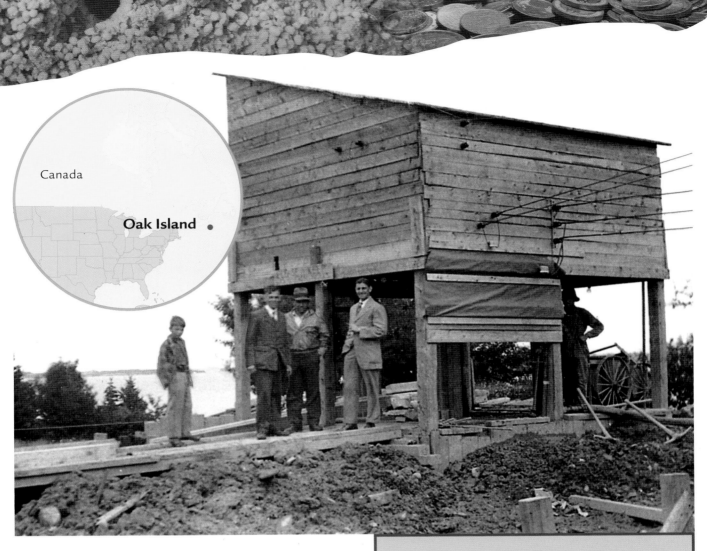

Canada

Oak Island •

Hopeful treasure hunters in 1931, beside the shaft of the Money Pit. A video taken inside the Money Pit in 1971 showed wooden chests, but the shaft collapsed before anyone could reach them.

HOT SPOTS

Alaric's soldiers used slaves to dig the bed of the Busento River and divert the water, so Alaric's body could be buried. To make sure no one told where Alaric's tomb was, the soldiers killed all the slaves when their work was done.

The Money Pit

Is there a fortune on Oak Island, Canada, or not? Treasure hunters have wasted many years looking for it. Their shaft, more than 200 feet (60 m) deep, is known as the Money Pit—not because it's full of treasure, but because digging it has cost so much money! They have dug through layers of timber, the sides of the shaft have collapsed, and it has flooded. But some still dream of finding treasure.

Egypt's treasures

When the pharaohs of ancient Egypt died, they were buried with everything they would need in the next life—including their most valuable and precious objects. Many people have dreamed of finding a pharaoh's tomb filled with treasure.

The gold funeral mask of Tutankhamun is decorated with priceless gems and colored glass.

Wonderful things

In 1922, archaeologist Howard Carter peered into the tomb of the ancient Egyptian pharaoh Tutankhamun, in the Valley of the Kings, and said he could see "wonderful things." Carter was about to uncover precious objects from 3,200 years ago. The greatest treasure was the pharaoh's gold mask, but there was also jewelry, a golden throne, a shrine, and statues.

HOT SPOTS

Tutankhamun's tomb was broken into by tomb robbers before it was discovered by Howard Carter. But they seem to have been stopped before they could steal any of its treasure.

Golden mummies

Bahariya Oasis • • Valley of the Kings
Egypt

In 1996, a donkey became stuck in a hole at the Bahariya Oasis in Egypt. Its owner climbed into the hole, and entered a tomb filled with 10,000 **mummies**. Many had masks covered in gold, so the **cemetery** became known as the Valley of the Golden Mummies. Although they were not buried with the "wonderful things" of a pharaoh, these mummies are among ancient Egypt's most amazing treasures.

The mummies seem to be arranged in family groups, with several generations buried together.

Ancient mummies
The mummies are about 2,000 years old

Pirate plunder

Imagine finding pirate treasure! Some people have, and the true stories of those who have spent years tracking it down are as exciting as the tales of the pirates themselves.

Black Sam's booty

In the early 1700s, the North American coast was terrorized by the pirate Sam Bellamy, also known as "Black Sam." In 1717, his ship, the *Whydah*, sank in a storm off Cape Cod, Massachusetts. Bellamy's loot of 180 bags of gold and silver coins vanished to the bottom of the sea. In 1984, Barry Clifford, a local treasure hunter, located the *Whydah*, but only 15,000 coins have been found so far. Clifford is convinced he will find all of Bellamy's **booty**.

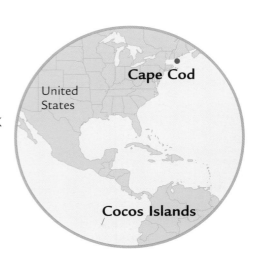

Gold jewelry found on the wreck of the *Whydah*.

Precious finds

A gold necklace, bracelets, and knee and elbow decorations, believed to have come from West Africa

Treasure island

In 1821, sailors on board the *Mary Dear* **mutinied** and stole the ship, which was on its way to Spain with a cargo of gold, silver, and jewels. The crew murdered the soldiers guarding the cargo and sailed to the Cocos Islands in the Pacific Ocean. Most of the crew was eventually captured and executed. There is a legend that a map exists, showing where the sailors buried the treasure before they were arrested, but no map has ever been found.

HOT SPOTS

The ship Queen Anne's Revenge *belonged to the fierce pirate Blackbeard. It ran aground off the coast of North Carolina in 1718. The ship was discovered in 1996, and more than 2,000 everyday objects have been found, but no treasure so far!*

Treasure chest

Pirate treasure is often said to be buried in chests

China's treasures

The amazing wealth of ancient China has recently been revealed, with fabulous discoveries of treasures buried long ago.

Each of the thousands of figures in the terra-cotta army was armed according to his rank.

Clay soldiers
The life-size figures are made from terra-cotta, a type of pottery

Terra-cotta army

One of the most remarkable buried treasures was found in 1974 at Xi'an, China. Archaeologists unvovered the tomb of the first Qin emperor and discovered more than 8,000 life-size figures of warriors and horses made from terra-cotta. The army of generals, soldiers, archers, cavalry, and chariots was buried in pits to guard the emperor's tomb.

China

Xi'an •

HOT SPOTS

According to stories, Emperor Qin Shi Huang-ti's tomb, 23 miles (35 km) east of Xi'an, contains booby traps and a map of China with rivers of mercury!

Suits of jade

Long ago, important people in China were buried in suits of **jade**. The first jade burial suits were discovered in 1968, in the tomb of Prince Liu Sheng and his wife, Lady Dou Wan, who died 2,100 years ago. Their bodies were covered in jade squares that had been sewn together with gold wire. Each suit was made from 2,500 pieces of jade and more than 2 pounds (1 kg) of gold.

Jade king

King Zhao Mo was buried in 122 B.C.

The jade suit of Zhao Mo, a king of early China. It is made from squares of jade tied together with red silk.

Roman riches

In Roman Britain, valuables were buried if their owners had to flee enemies. Some people did not return, so the goods stayed hidden until they were found many years later.

The Mildenhall treasure

About 1,600 years ago, a rich Roman buried 34 silver dishes, bowls, and spoons in Mildenhall, UK. He never went back for them, and these valuable objects stayed in the ground until 1943, when a farmer dug them up by accident. The most stunning piece is the Great Dish, which is made from silver and measures 2 feet (60 cm) in diameter.

United Kingdom

•• **Hoxne**

Mildenhall

The Great Dish from the Mildenhall treasure. It was probably made in the eastern Mediterranean and is one of the finest examples of Roman silver ever found.

Staring face
At the center is Oceanus, god of the ocean

Dancing figures
Around the edge are dancing figures and creatures from Roman **mythology**

Gold and silver coins

In 1992, Eric Lawes was using a **metal detector** to search for a hammer in a field at Hoxne (say: hox-on), UK. Instead of the lost hammer, his machine detected Roman treasure—200 gold and silver objects and 14,780 coins! There were gold chains, finger rings and bracelets, a silver tigress, a pepperbox, bowls, and spoons. Ten spoons had the name Aurelius Ursicinus on them, who may have been the original Roman owner.

HOT SPOTS

Both the Mildenhall treasure and the Hoxne treasure are on display at the British Museum in London.

Heads up

Portraits of Roman emperors appear on the "heads" side of the coins

Some of the thousands of gold and silver coins from the Hoxne treasure.

Lost ships

Finding a lost ship is an exciting way to discover treasure. One of the most famous treasures from a ship was found on dry land, not at the bottom of the sea.

Burial boat

One of England's first kings might have been buried in a boat. He was King Raedwald, who died in about A.D. 625. Some believe that a boat found inside a mound at Sutton Hoo, UK, in 1939 is his grave. The boat and the body had rotted away, but his treasure was still there. Archaeologists found a warrior's helmet and weapons, gold coins from France, and silver bowls from the Mediterranean.

Sweden

United Kingdom

Stockholm Harbor

Sutton Hoo

Helmet
Reconstruction of the Sutton Hoo helmet

Buckle
Gold belt buckle from Sutton Hoo

The valuable objects found at Sutton Hoo suggest they belonged to a king.

Raising the *Vasa*

Carpenters, painters, and sculptors spent years working on the **Vasa** warship, the pride of the Swedish navy. As it sailed out of the harbor on its first voyage in 1628, a light wind caught its sails. The ship leaned to the left, water rushed in through the **gun ports**, and it sank. Divers recovered 53 of its 64 guns. The ship was then abandoned until 1961, when more than 15,000 objects were discovered. It was a treasure trove of items used by sailors in the seventeenth century. Even a tub of butter was found!

The *Vasa* is the only warship from the 1600s to be seen anywhere in the world. The hull is covered with hundreds of sculptures.

HOT SPOTS

The wreck of the Vasa lay undisturbed just outside Stockholm Harbor for 333 years. No one really knows why the ship sank but historians think that the beautiful golden carvings were so heavy that the ship was unbalanced. When a gust of wind caught the sails, the Vasa toppled over and sank.

21

Viking valuables

On their journeys to Europe, North Africa, and the Middle East, the Vikings collected gold and silver. Sometimes they buried their treasure, and it is these **hoards** that treasure hunters find today.

Treasure chest

In 1840, workmen repairing the banks of the Ribble River, in northern England, found Europe's largest hoard of Viking silver—7,500 silver coins and 1,000 silver ingots and pieces of silver. It weighed 88 pounds (40 kg) and was buried in a lead chest. Known as the Cuerdale hoard, it was buried by Vikings in about A.D. 905. Historians believe that the treasure may have been buried by soldiers for safety.

Sweden
United Kingdom
Tureholm
Timboholm
Isle of Man
Cuerdale

Silver coins and strips of twisted silver from the Viking Cuerdale hoard.

22

Spirals
More than 20 gold spirals were found

Heavy hoard
The treasure weighed 15.5 pounds (7 kg) and included gold buckles, rings, and ingots

Part of the treasure found at Timboholm. So far, this is the largest hoard of gold discovered in Sweden.

Hundreds of hoards

In 1774, Viking gold jewelry was found at Tureholm, Sweden. Sadly, most of it was melted down. In recent times, hoards have gone to museums, such as the gold ingots and **spirals** found at Timboholm, Sweden, in 1904. They belonged to a Viking goldsmith, who buried his raw material for safekeeping. The first Viking hoard from the Netherlands was found in 1996, and in 2003, silver coins and ingots were found on the Isle of Man.

HOT SPOTS
In 2004, two amateur treasure hunters discovered a gold ring in a field with their metal detectors. It had been lost by its owner in either the ninth or tenth century and had been buried ever since.

Wealth of South America

The lure of gold once drew treasure hunters from Europe to South America. But the illegal work of modern-day raiders has done much to uncover the continent's buried treasure.

The legend of El Dorado

When the Spaniards first explored South America, they heard about a chief who covered himself in gold dust, then washed it off in a lake. From this came the legend of El Dorado (Spanish for "the gilded one"). Treasure hunters have searched for the golden kingdom, but all have returned empty-handed. However, there is some truth behind the legend. In Colombia, chiefs of the Muisca people really did coat themselves in gold dust before diving into Lake Guatavita.

Treasure hunters tried to drain Lake Guatavita by cutting a deep notch at the side of the lake.

The Lord of Sipán

When **looters** dug into an ancient tomb at Sipán, Peru, they found gold objects made by the Moche people, 1,500 years ago. Archaeologists heard about the site, and in 1987, they discovered a tomb missed by the robbers. It was the tomb of a warrior priest, the Lord of Sipán. Inside were feather headdresses, clothes, beaded ornaments, gold jewelry, and a gold headdress.

HOT SPOTS

The remains of guards in the Lord of Sipán's tomb were found with their feet cut off. Historians think this was to make sure they did not run away and leave the king unguarded in the next life.

The Lord of Sipán's tomb was the first intact royal tomb of the Moche people to have been found and studied.

Grave finds

Two male guards and three women were buried with the Lord of Sipán

Buried cities

Long ago, the rivers of Iraq changed course and cities became deserts. In Italy, a volcano destroyed Roman towns. These disasters hid treasures for us to uncover today.

Royal cemetery of Ur

British archaeologist Leonard Woolley found some spectacular treasures at Ur, an ancient city in southern Iraq. In the 1920s, he found a cemetery with tombs of kings and queens that was about 4,500 years old. The rulers were buried with priceless objects, including a golden ram caught in a bush, a king's gold helmet, and a queen's gold headdress. A lyre (a harp-like instrument) and a decorated board for playing games were among the many other treasures found in the **royal cemetery**.

Golden ram
The goat's fleece is made from shells, and its skin is gold leaf

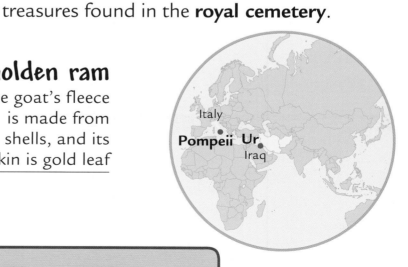

Italy

Pompeii **Ur**

Iraq

The golden ram from Ur is one of the most famous finds from the ancient city. The ram may have been used to support a bowl.

City of ash

The volcano Vesuvius erupted in A.D. 79 and destroyed the Roman town of Pompeii, Italy. The town vanished beneath a deep layer of ash. The first **excavations** at Pompeii took place in the 1700s, and work on the site continues today. Building by building, street by street, the ruins are being uncovered, revealing a complete Roman town that is one of the greatest treasures of the ancient world.

Many of the houses in Pompeii had mosaics on the floor, such as this one of a guard dog.

The ancient Roman town of Pompeii, with the volcano Vesuvius in the background.

HOT SPOTS

Hoards of Roman treasures have been found in and around Pompeii. These were all lost on August 24, A.D. 79, when Vesuvius blew its top.

Finding treasure today

It is everyone's dream to find treasure—and for some people, this dream comes true. The discovery of treasure makes news headlines, but not always for the right reasons.

The lure of treasure

Some modern treasure hunters steal from tombs, shipwrecks, buried cities, and even museums. They break the law, and many also damage precious, historic places. But not all treasure hunters are like this. Archaeologists discover treasure all the time, and what they find does not have to be gold or silver to be valuable. Broken pots, pieces of bone, and bits of buildings are their treasure, which they use to help them find out more about the past.

Archaeologists are careful to record everything they find. Here, an archaeologist is using a grid to help him make an accurate drawing of two pots buried inside a circle of stones.

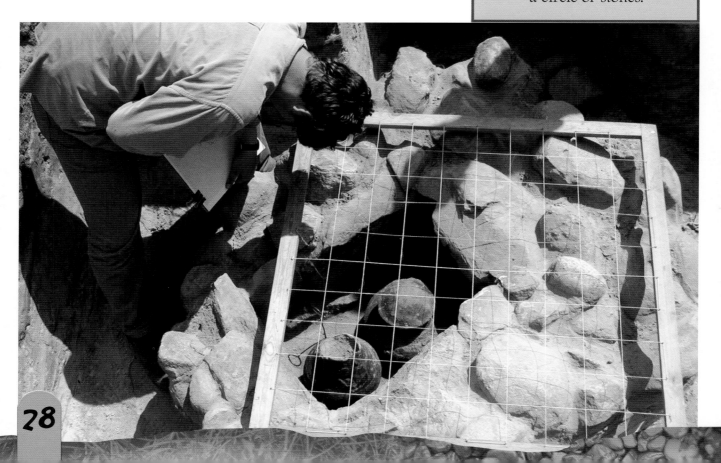

Field of gold

In 1948, three hoards of gold **torcs** were found in a field at Snettisham, UK. Two years later, more were found in the same field. Then in 1990, 50 more torcs, 70 rings and bracelets, and some coins were found with a metal detector. The field of gold held even more surprises, because archaeologists then found another five hoards of gold, silver, and bronze torcs! The Snettisham torcs are about 2,000 years old.

United Kingdom

Snettisham

Some of the gold and silver torcs found at Snettisham in 1990.

Tangled torcs

The soil was removed from around the torcs before they were lifted from the ground

Glossary

archaeologists People who study the remains of the past.

booty Stolen goods.

burial mound A small hill made of soil, built over the burial place of a dead person.

cemetery A place where human or animal remains are buried.

cremated Burned a dead body to ashes.

excavations Archaeological sites where earth is dug and removed in an organized way to discover information or treasure.

galleon A large sailing ship, used by Spain in the fifteenth and sixteenth centuries.

gun ports Openings in a ship through which the cannons are fired.

hoards Hidden stores of valuable goods.

ingots Rectangular blocks of metal, especially gold or silver.

jade A hard stone, usually green in color, that is carved to make jewelry and other items.

looters People who steal objects from an ancient site to sell them.

metal detector A machine used to search for metal objects buried in the ground.

mummies The preserved bodies of dead people or animals.

mutinied Rebelled against their captain or commanding officers.

mythology A collection of stories or traditions that may mix up facts and fiction.

myrtle A flowering evergreen shrub.

pharaohs Rulers or god-kings of ancient Egypt.

porcelain A type of fine pottery, first made in China.

royal cemetery A place where kings, queens, and other members of a ruling family are buried.

salvage operation The recovery of cargo from the wreck of a ship, soon after it has sunk.

spirals Gold shaped into bracelets and rings.

tombs Places where people are buried. They may (or may not) contain treasure.

torcs Large metal rings, made from gold, silver, or bronze, worn around the neck.

treasure An object, or objects, of great value.

treasure hunters People who search for treasure. Some treasure hunters damage ancient sites and break the law in their search for treasure. Others work with archaeologists.

Index

Web sites

http://ina.tamu.edu/ub_main.htm   The *Uluburun* shipwreck, one of the world's oldest wrecks.

www.vocshipwrecks.nl/home_voyages3/geldermalsen.html   The *Geldermalsen* and its cargo of Chinese porcelain.

www.vasamuseet.se/Home/Vasamuseet/Om.aspx   The *Vasa* shipwreck.

www.archaeology.co.uk/ca/timeline/saxon/suttonhoo/ship/suttonhoo.htm   The Sutton Hoo treasure.

www.mildenhallmuseum.co.uk/mildenhall_treasure.htm   The Mildenhall treasure.

www.unmuseum.org/oakisl.htm   The Oak Island Money Pit.